Life is short so..
scratch hard,

LIFE AMONG THE GIANTS

To Mary Doll.
Enjoy The Book.

JMBall

Life Among the Giants

the

Giants

Living with Newfoundland Dogs

William Ball

Belleville, Ontario, Canada

Life Among the Giants

Copyright © 2008, William Ball

Illustrated by Marja Heikkila
Edited by Birgit Schultz

ISBN: 978-1-55452-327-6

**For more information or
to order additional copies, please contact:**

William Ball
Email: info@lifeamongthegiants.com
Website: www.lifeamongthegiants.com

Epic Press is an imprint of *Essence Publishing,* a Christian Book Publisher dedicated to furthering the work of Christ through the written word. For more information, contact:
20 Hanna Court, Belleville, Ontario, Canada K8P 5J2
Phone: 1-800-238-6376 • Fax: (613) 962-3055
E-mail: info@essence-publishing.com
Web site: www.essence-publishing.com

This book is dedicated to Altesse Kelsey, our dear and departed golden retriever, a great, gentle dog who spent the last two years of her life learning to coexist with two 150-pound Newfoundland dogs. She welcomed our first gentle giant into her house with disdain in the beginning but eventually with love and acceptance.

Kelsey, the Golden Newf

I love my dogs, This is their home,
From which I hope, They'll never roam,
They're faithful friends
I love them best—This is their home
You are the guest.
If dogs to you, Are just a peeve
Then by all means, feel free to leave!

-author unknown

Table of Contents

Acknowledgements

Thank you to marilyn Lees, a dear friend who convinced me that there was indeed a book to be written.

Many thanks to my wife, Ingrid, for her contagious excitement for the idea of putting these memories on paper and her invaluable help in remembering the important Newf events in our life. To our children, Danny, David and Tammy, who many times during these past fifteen years must have thought that their parents had flipped over the edge, but nevertheless still visited our clan and endured the drool and the ubiquitous Newf hair without a complaint. (Well, maybe a few!)

I would also like to thank Fran and Keith Ledingham and Lars and Marij Erup for their help and suggestions. They have been dear friends ever since day one with our Newfs. Fran currently owns Goldie and Georgy Girl, who are mother and sister to one of our girls, Molly, and is always thinking of adding to her troop. Lars and Marij are owned by a wonderful Newf girl named Naja. Thanks also to a good friend, Tina

Barton, for all of her help and suggestions. Tina is owned by two charming Newf girls, Caera and Misha, who happen to be daughters of another of our Newfs, Rimshot.

Editing by Birgit Schultz and illustrations by Marja Heikkila were done on the basis of friendship and are very much appreciated.

Very special thanks to our dear friend and Newf breeder Nina Coté. Nina runs Marcarpents Kennels in Ontario, Canada, and throughout these years has been a mine of information in our learning about this wonderful breed of dog. Without Nina's friendship and generosity, our life with Newfs would have been vastly different.

And of course, thanks to all of our other Newf friends who have made this journey with the Newfoundland dog so enjoyable and memorable.

THE NEWFOUNDLAND

The newfoundland is a large, usually black, breed of dog originally used as a working dog in Newfoundland. They are known for their sweet dispositions, loyalty, and natural water rescue tendencies. The Newfoundland dog excels at water rescue, due partly to their webbed feet and amazing swimming abilities.

Weight:	100-220 pounds (45-100 kg)
Height:	25-29 inches (63-74 cm)
Coat:	black, landseer (black and white), grey, and brown
Activity level:	low–high (large range of activity levels, especially between younger–older)
Learning rate:	mid high
Temperament:	some individual changes in temperament: submissive–stubborn, passive–courageous, patient
Guard dog ability:	average–mid high
Watch-dog ability:	med
Litter size:	8-10
Life span:	9-10 years

The breed originated in Newfoundland from a breed indigenous to the island that later became known as the St. John's Dog. The speculation they may be partly descended from the big black bear dogs introduced by the Vikings in 1001 A.D. is based more in romance than in fact. It is more likely that their size results from the introduction of large mastiffs brought to the island by many generations of Portuguese fishermen, who had been visiting Newfoundland since the 1400s. By the time colonization was permitted in 1610, the distinct physical characteristics and mental attributes had been established in the breed. In the early 1880s, fishermen from Ireland and England described two main types of working dog: one more heavily built, large with a longish coat, whereas the other was lighter in build, an active, smooth-coated water dog. The heavier one was the Newfoundland and the other was then known as the Lesser St. John's Dog, the forerunner of the Labrador Retriever. The dogs were used in similar ways to pull fishnets and heavy equipment.[1]

This is a large and very powerful dog but is known as a gentle giant because of its mild, friendly and loyal personality. Even though the Newf is of a calm disposition and has a very laid-back character, it can be a challenge to own one. It can be a high maintenance dog and because of the drool and shedding is not meant for the family that is obsessed with neatness. Newfoundlands require grooming on a regular basis, and because of the

---

[1] Wikipedia, The Free Encyclopedia, "Newfoundland (dog)," http://en.wikipedia.org/wiki/Newfoundland_(dog) (accessed May 2008).

almost constant shedding, one must possess a very good quality vacuum cleaner. It goes without saying that as the number of Newfs in the household increases, so does the energy and time required to provide the care they need and deserve. During most of the past thirteen years we have had more than one of these gentle beasts living with us at the same time, and presently we have four.

My intention in writing this book is to give an insight into how the Newfoundland dog fits into the family home environment. Needless to say, when one has four large dogs living in the house the tendency is to take many photos. I have included several of these pictures throughout the book, which will help readers to visualize the unique atmosphere in the home.

We became interested in Newfoundland dogs quite by accident. We had heard of them and had seen the typical photos of them standing on a Newfoundland shore staring out over the sea. However, we really did not know much about them. Our "dog" life before Newfs consisted of many mixed breeds, mostly from shelters, and one purebred golden retriever by the name of Kelsey. None of our dogs of the past ever weighed more than sixty pounds.

One morning, many years ago, not far from our house and at the beginning of our commute to work, Ingrid and I passed a couple walking a monstrous black dog along the side of the road. We were quite impressed with this animal even from a distance. We saw them often during the next few weeks and became determined to meet them and discover more about this noble looking dog. Eventually it became too difficult to just drive by, so one day we stopped and said hello and were introduced to Charlie, the Newfoundland. Charlie, a very large, old and docile male Newf, was a rescue dog. During the next few weeks we met them many more times and learned of the qualities of this breed of dog. We learned of their gentleness, kindness and loyalty to their owners and became determined to eventually have one of our own.

My goodness! What a coincidence! Within weeks, while at our local post office, I noticed a homemade sign on the bulletin board advertising Newfoundland puppies for sale. This, to our way of thinking, was just too good to be true. I made note of the phone number, and the next day we were there looking at the last two remaining pups from the litter. We made our choice, and two weeks later our life among the giants began.

Our Original Gaggle of Newfs

This first section of the book will present Kelsey, Murphy, Bailey and Enchantee. The arrival of these dogs into our life and some of the exploits of these first years introduced us to life among the giants.

Altesse Kelsey: Newf Wannabe

Kelsey was approaching old age. For the past twelve years this beautiful golden retriever had lived a life of leisure and enjoyment. She had been an only dog all of her life, so she was able to awake each morning at her chosen hour, greet the humans in her life and receive a morning treat and many scratches and hugs. Often she would wander the neighbourhood, visiting friends down the street who would give her left-over muffins from their breakfasts. She would finish her rounds, then come home and lie out on the back deck for a while, looking down at the creek. In the winter after-noons, perhaps she would walk down the frozen creek to visit a couple of dog friends and watch the children play hockey on the ice. Suppertime would see her back at the house, where her dinner was never late and always enjoyed. Evenings were spent by the fire with the family, then to sleep for the night at the foot of the humans' bed. She had always been a gentle, easygoing dog, who had bonded very closely to the two-legged members of the family.

All in all she had a great life. Now at twelve years old she was starting to slow down a bit and seemed to enjoy the quiet times more often.

Murphy-The Intruder

To her dismay, one day a little black firestorm in the form of a Newf puppy named Murphy made his appearance. Suddenly Kelsey's life was uprooted from her peaceful existence to one of constant hectic activity. This little black furball, who at nine weeks of age already weighed twenty pounds, spent every waking moment zipping around the house, over this, under that and never too far from wherever Kelsey was trying to relax. Kelsey's first reaction was one of disdain, ignoring this little creature (or trying to). Then came the discipline period, where she attempted to set this boisterous little guy straight as to who was the boss around here. And Murphy learned quickly.

The first lesson was on his first night out of the crate when he was allowed to sleep in the bedroom with the rest of the family. He came into the bedroom with us and promptly took up a spot on the floor at the foot of the bed. He was innocently unaware (or maybe he just didn't care) that this was Kelsey's sleeping area. Several minutes later, Kelsey entered the room as usual and paused at the door, glaring at this nervy newcomer. She then rushed over to him, making quite a fuss, barking ferociously in his face, and he wasted no time making his escape. This was our first experience seeing any aggressiveness from Kelsey in all of the twelve years she had been with us. We never forgot it, and the intimidated Murphy never again slept in that particular spot.

At this point in our life, my mom was in her seventies and living with Ingrid, me, Kelsey and Murphy, the exuberant little ten- or twelve-week-old terror. Mom was not too steady on her feet but was never bothered by Kelsey, who was a senior citizen herself and was also slow in getting around. But this Murphy guy had no respect for old age. He would tear around the house, run up behind Mom, grab the hem of her housecoat and try to charge off running in the opposite direction. Mom was a true dog lover, but sometimes this little guy was just too much. When she was coming out of her room in the morning, she would stay hidden at first and call to us, asking if Murphy was around before venturing out. Many times we found Murphy lying in wait around the corner, and when she made an appearance he would charge out from his spot and grab that hem. We all enjoyed those times immensely, including Mom, although she never admitted it.

This little furry puppy very quickly grew into an impressive 150-pound gentle giant who towered over the 50-pound Kelsey. But Kelsey's training had been a success. She was the boss, and Murphy knew it. Kelsey's energy level also increased dramatically. She seemed to hurtle into her second childhood with a vigour she had not shown for years. As the weeks went by, the relationship grew, and a tight bond was established between the two dogs. Hours were spent playing tug-of-war, and wrestling matches dominated the evenings. With every game played, the winner was never in doubt. Kelsey always came out on top. She always won the tugs-of-war and consistently won the wrestling matches by ending up on top of Murphy with her teeth wrapped around his throat. Both dogs relished these times, and the relationship flourished.

Murphy now joined Kelsey in her wanderings down the creek in the winter to join in with the children and other dogs on the ice. It was as if Kelsey was showing him the ropes. They would frolic away from home for a while, then run back, often bringing along one of the other dogs, usually another golden, to play around here for a while. Then back down the creek.

These activities, however, did not take place during the summer season because without the frozen creek there was no way for them to get across. During the spring and fall the ice is often not thick enough to hold a 150-pound dog, as Murph discovered one late fall day. I was in the house; the dogs were in the backyard. Every few minutes I would look out to make sure the two were okay. At one point I looked out and could see only Kelsey standing on the dock. I heard Murphy's crying coming from somewhere and when I went to the dock discovered that he had tried to cross the ice and had gone through. He was swimming in circles in the middle of the creek. Every time he tried to climb out, the ice would break and he would fall back in. So, what to do? I knew immediately that I was going for a winter swim. I walked out on the ice and waited to go through. What a terrible feeling, but once in the water the duty at hand made me forget about the cold. I hoisted him up onto the shore, and off he ran with Kelsey as if nothing had happened. I, on the other hand, was soaked through and shivering uncontrollably. However, this was a small price to pay to save our boy.

Every now and then something will happen that teaches us about another quality of these dogs, previously unknown. One of these incidents occurred one day when I was out in the woods with Kelsey and Murphy. At the time Kelsey was about thirteen years old and Murphy was a young, healthy 150-pound boy. We were walking in an old park of about 100 acres, which had been abandoned for several years and was now almost back to its natural state with overgrown trails and roads. Water inlets and streams wind their way through this "paradise," and the abundant wildlife is everywhere. On this particular day the three of us were making our way through the long grass and shrubs between a stream on one side and a heavily wooded area on the other.

At one point I realized that the dogs were not with me, and I turned around to go back to see where they were. As I was making my way back, I came upon a huge deer, a mature buck, standing at the edge of the wooded area. I was very close to him, about twenty feet, but he had not seen me. I stopped and stood very still, just watching him as he slowly crossed in front of me, making his way to the water. This was an amazing sight, and for the moment I had forgotten about the dogs. Then, to my amazement, emerging from the woods, from the same spot as the deer and about ten feet behind him, strolled Kelsey and Murphy, very calmly, seeming to not even notice this huge animal in front of them. As I watched, the deer slowly turned away from me and wandered up along the waterway and the dogs turned towards me. We three then turned and continued our walk in the opposite direction. Needless to say, I could not understand what had just happened. Why these two dogs had reacted the way they did, which was no reaction at all, is a mystery to me. It was as if this was a most normal occurrence, nothing out of the ordinary, something that happens every day.

Kelsey and murph

Quiet moment with murphy

Bailey-The Food Disposal System

After a few months, along came Bailey! We found Bailey at a shelter in Montreal, Quebec. He was four years old, 160 pounds and had been given up for adoption by his owners, who could no longer keep him. When we first saw him at the shelter he was a mess physically and extremely depressed at being abandoned in a strange and noisy place. We decided immediately that he had to come home with us. The shelter gave us some information about him before we left. One of his major preferences, apparently, was toast and cheese. Little did we know how significant this tidbit of information would turn out to be.

When we arrived home, poor Bailey was greeted with complete indifference by Kelsey and an immediate lesson from Murphy as to where Bailey's place was to be in the hierarchy of the group. Bailey was destined to be at the bottom of the ladder. After a couple of months of some noisy but harmless episodes, things settled into the routine the three dogs had set: Kelsey number one, Murphy number two, and at the bottom was Bailey. All seemed happy with this arrangement, and our group got along famously.

We started learning about Bailey's special talents and determination very quickly. In 1997 an event took place where many Newf owners and their dogs made a trek across Canada and the United States to Newfoundland to celebrate the 500th anniversary of John Cabot's arrival. This trek was scheduled to travel the Trans-Canada Highway and pass by close to our house on Bailey's second day with us. We had planned on meeting this group of owners and their Newfs at a nearby service centre but decided to leave Bailey at home for him to adjust to his surroundings. Therefore, the day before Bailey's arrival, I built a large pen measuring about ten feet by twelve feet in our backyard. I used four-by-four posts, with two-by-four and one-by-three framing. It was quite an impressive structure (I thought), and we felt Bailey would be happy in his little area for a couple of hours until our return. Shortly after his arrival at our home we decided to see how he liked the pen. We led him in and closed the gate. We then left him and walked up onto the deck about twenty feet away. Within minutes, he was standing next to us and the "impressive" structure that I had spent a full day constructing was in shambles. Two-by-four and one-by-three boards were lying all over the ground. We had discovered just how much Bailey loved being with his humans. The result of this was twofold: the rest of the pen was dismantled the next day, and Bailey accompanied us to meet the Newf Trek that afternoon.

At this same time, my father was visiting from Vancouver, spending a couple of weeks with us. My father was *not* a dog person. He really could not understand us having a golden retriever *and* a Newfoundland. This was beyond his comprehension, but he endured quite admirably during the time he was with us. As it turned out, we were due to pick up Bailey from the shelter the day after my dad arrived. While I drove the sixty miles to pick him up, Ingrid stayed at home with the other dogs and my dad and explained to him that I had gone to pick up a dog from the shelter that needed a temporary home, so he would stay with us until a permanent home was found (which was our original intention). When I arrived back home with this 160-pound Newf, who was in terrible shape, not having been groomed for several months, I had the feeling that my dad wanted to deny our father-son connection. At one point we were all on the deck with Kelsey and Murphy and this new interloper sticking his curious nose everywhere. Within minutes Murphy took it upon himself to show this intruder just who was boss around here. Noise and confusion reigned for a couple of minutes, but no one was hurt—except me, who got in the way and received a nip on my arm. Dad's reaction? "You're not going to keep this dog, are you?"

"No," I said, "just until we find him a good home."

The next day was the day we were going to meet the Newf Trek people. So off we went, Ingrid, Lars, who was also visiting, my dad, Murphy and Bailey. Among the Newf Trek group was a fellow who is involved in Newf Rescue, so we were anxious to talk to him. After introducing Bailey to Lloyd and asking if he thought we would have problems placing him, his reply was, "I don't think this guy is going anywhere," and he was right. It was that day that we decided that Bailey will stay with us. Obviously, we were hesitant to break this news to Dad, but we did, and he seemed to take it quite well. However, for that first week, Bailey slept in the porch as a buffer from Murph until all were a little more comfortable with each other. I should add that Ingrid felt so sorry for this big guy sleeping alone in a strange place that she would spend about an hour each evening before he went to sleep singing lullabies to him. We have never been too free with this particular piece of information, but now it's out there.

When a dog owner takes his dog for a walk on leash, it can be a meaningful bonding experience for both human and dog. There is nothing quite like a peaceful walk along a country road with a couple of Newfs on leash. However, when those two Newfs each weigh 150 to 160 pounds, are healthy and strong and one of them has never seen a cow, that walk can become an experience one never forgets. This walk took place during the first two weeks of Bailey's arrival. It never occurred to us that Bailey, having lived in the big city for the first four years of his life, had never experienced country living and the everyday things we take for granted. I had Murphy and Bailey each on a leash, and we were casually strolling a quiet country road when we passed by a field where the farmer was keeping ten or fifteen young calves.

Murphy, accustomed to country living as he was, never took notice of these little creatures, but Bailey, as soon as he caught a glimpse of them, lost control and charged off the road towards the fenced area. Murphy, upon seeing this, figured that he had better panic as well, so they both charged off the road towards these unsuspecting calves. As luck would have it, this road was bordered by a deep eight-foot gully on each side. As anyone can imagine, one 180-pound human is no match for 300 pounds of Newfoundland dogs, both bent on getting somewhere quickly. I was dragged, on my stomach, down one side of this gully and up the other before I could regain control of these two obsessed steam engines.

All this was taking place amidst loud barking from the dogs and me yelling at them to stop. It was a confusing scene, to say the least. It all came to an end when we reached the fence at the top of the other side of the gully. I was able to regain control and coerce them back up to the road, where we proceeded to continue our walk. The front of my body was covered with dirt and grass, and I had scraped knees. About fifty feet down the road at a railway crossing sitting in his truck was a railway worker, who had apparently been watching the whole incident. As I walked by, looking like a survivor from a war battle, he gave me a friendly wave, which I returned, but neither of us spoke about what had just transpired. This was powerful motivation to begin serious leash training and "cow socialization" the next day.

Newfoundland dogs love the water. Our property is bordered on two sides by a creek that is about twenty feet wide and five to six feet deep. In the middle of the summer there is quite a lot of algae and other green vegetation in the water. One day, our neighbours living on the other side of the creek were having a barbecue with some guests, and they were all gathered in their backyard cooking and socializing, lots of laughter and kids running around. Bailey was a social guy who loved children, and as soon as he spotted the kids, he charged into the water, swam to the other side and ran to join in the fun. However, he was dripping wet and was covered in green "stuff" from the creek. As we all know, a dog's instinct when getting out of water is to shake. However, Bailey waited until he was in the midst of all the happy barbecuers before giving a few good shakes and spreading this mixture all over anyone nearby. Luckily everyone was having such a good time that they all laughed about it. It took a concerted effort from all of us to convince him to swim back home.

The above incidents all took place within the first two weeks of Bailey moving in with us, so we were understandably curious as to what our life was going to be like with this fellow and wondering if we had made the right decision in bringing him home. However, once he settled in and learned a few rules of the house, his wonderful personality blossomed and he turned out to be a great, loyal companion to all of us.

This section could easily have been called "How to Train the Humans," for when one owns a Newfoundland dog, especially more than one, the humans of the group undergo as much training as the dogs. With Bailey we discovered this fact quite quickly. In the write-up we received from the shelter at the time of adoption, the previous owners mentioned that his favourite treat was toast and cheese. The fact that food was mentioned here was not by accident. Bailey turned out to be a 160-pound food disposal system. For the next year or so we never ceased to be amazed at some of the tricks he would use to get food—any type of food.

Several times we came home from spending a short time away only to discover the amazing talents this boy possessed. There was the time we found the peels from a couple of bananas on the dining room floor. He had actually managed to peel each banana, eat the inside and leave the peels on the floor. We had bought a dozen pears and had left them in a bowl on the dining room table. Neither of us had eaten any of them, but suddenly they were nowhere to be found. Bailey's talents did not occur to us until a couple of days later when we found some of the pear stems hidden under the table. Mystery solved.

We own a ceramic cookie jar in the shape of Daffy Duck. It stands about eighteen inches tall, the top five inches being Daffy's head. The head is the removable top of the jar. This is not a dog cookie jar but rather one for human treats. It is certainly not a centrepiece of our house but has a commanding presence on the kitchen counter. One day, upon returning home from another of our short excursions, we noticed Daffy's head on the kitchen counter, but no jar. We found the body sitting upright on the dining room floor. The jar was now empty of the cookies, but our disposal system had left a half inch of drool covering the bottom. We never did figure out how he managed to remove the ceramic head and leave it on the counter and carry the body all the way to the dining room for his snack without breaking anything.

Often I would take Murphy and Bailey grocery shopping in the van. All of our dogs have always loved going for rides, and these were great times to get them into town for some socializing. On one such road trip I had picked up a few things at one store and then stopped at another for a few more supplies. After being in the store for only about five minutes, I heard, "The person who owns a tan-coloured van in the parking lot, please come to the front of the store." Waiting for me at the door was an elderly gentleman, who told me I should check the dogs in the van. As I walked up to the driver's door, there was Bailey, sitting in the driver's seat looking out the window at me as I approached. He was covered from head to foot with cake crumbs. When I opened the door I found that the complete interior of the van was also covered with crumbs. The only clean area I could find was in the far rear corner of the van. Sitting in this spotless area was Murphy, himself also spotless. He made sure that I knew he had been sitting there, innocently watching Bailey as he devoured a complete lemon pound cake that I had hidden under the front seat. The look on his face seemed to say, "Don't look at me! It was him."

It is natural for owners of one breed of dog to band together because of common interests and social events. We have been very fortunate that the relationships we have developed because of the Newfoundland dog have been with wonderful people who have become our very good friends. We enjoy many social times together with all of our dogs. Two of these very good friends also had two Newfs at the time of this incident, and we spent many hours together enjoying the companionship of our "horde" of Newfoundland dogs. Quite quickly these friends, Lars and Marij, became familiar with Bailey's talents in obtaining food. This was demonstrated one evening when we were all at their house for dinner. While we humans ate our meal, the dogs were lying around the house, mostly in the dining area where the food was located. Following the meal, we adjourned to the living room, where we enjoyed a dessert and some after-dinner treats. As we sat around talking and enjoying one another's company, Bailey lay not too far from the living room table from where these treats were beckoning. He never indicated that he was even thinking about them. At the end of the evening as we were leaving, we were putting on our coats at the door with the dogs at our feet, and as we started outside Bailey suddenly turned around, made a mad dash back into the living room, grabbed a mouthful of treats off the table and promptly came back to the door, looking very satisfied with himself. Knowledge of his talents spread quickly amongst our Newf friends.

Bloat is a condition that may occur in deep-chested animals such as horses and some breeds of dogs. It is medical condition where the stomach becomes overextended by excessive gas. If the animal does not receive a vet's attention fairly quickly (within a couple of hours), the stomach may twist and cut off blood supply to other organs. Most often, this is fatal. The vet must make an incision and physically untwist the stomach and put it back into its normal position.

About one year after Bailey came to live with us, he bloated. Luckily, at the time we were subscribed to Newf-L, which is an Internet mailing list where Newf owners gather and discuss common interests and share Newf stories. In the few weeks prior to Bailey bloating, the list had been discussing bloat and the symptoms. Because of this, bloat was fresh in our minds. Therefore we were lucky enough to recognize his condition and rushed him to our vet, and all turned out well.

The symptoms may be some or all of the following:

• Attempting to vomit (usually unsuccessful)
• Anxiety and restlessness (can't lie down, can't stand still, some pacing)
• Hunched-up appearance
• Bloated abdomen; may feel tight, like a drum

If there is one positive thing that came from this scary and painful (for Bailey) experience, it is that it led us to meet and become close friends with Nina and Marc Cote. When Bailey came home from the vet, his complete underside had been shaved for the surgery. The first thing we noticed was his tattoo, which previously had been covered by his thick coat. This piqued our interest in trying to find out a bit about his past and which breeder he came from. We found Marcarpents Kennels through an Internet search and e-mailed the lady in question (Nina) and asked if she knew how we could trace the tattoo number to the appropriate breeder. To our surprise she wrote back and informed us that this number was hers—and she lived only five miles from us. Needless to say we were quite anxious to take Bailey for a visit. Upon our arrival at the kennel there was a very happy meeting between breeder and Newf and also the beginning of a long friendship with us. This turned out to be a major event in our "Newf life" because since then, all of our Newfs have come from this kennel.

Bailey-one week before we lost him

Soon after Bailey's arrival, Kelsey's age caught up with her. It was a sad day when we had to say goodbye. This loss obviously affected our family but surprisingly affected Murphy as well. For a couple of weeks he showed very little energy and spent most of his time lying on the chesterfield, gazing out the living room window up the street. It was heartbreaking to see but was a necessary part of the healing process for him.

Around this time we spent a couple of summers holidaying in New Brunswick, along the shores of the Bay of Fundy. During these years we had a cabin on the shore and we would spend a week enjoying the ocean with the two Newfs. As much as they enjoyed the time there, they were still not home and in their normal routine, so most of the time they never strayed too far from Ingrid or me. This desire to be close to us was shown day and night. This was a nice little cabin, with the emphasis on the word *little*, especially concerning the bedroom. This room was so small that when you walked through the door you had less than two feet before you were at the bed, and it was the same distance from the other side of the bed to the far wall. We enjoyed about three feet from bed to wall at the foot of the bed. This was a small room.

It just happened that the times we spent there were usually very hot and humid nights. There was no air conditioning, so it was like trying to sleep in a sauna on many nights. These dogs could have slept out in the spacious living room, which had many open windows and offered some relief from the discomfort, but nope! The two of them, not wanting to be too far from their humans, would squeeze their 150- and 160-pound bodies into these cramped quarters to sleep. Those claustrophobic nights were memorable ones. Trying to sleep with these two snoring on the floor and the coyotes howling down the shore was almost impossible. You have to love these dogs to live with them!

murphy, alone now, seeming to be missing Bailey

Enchantee—The "Collector"

After about one year with Murphy and Bailey, the chance came for us to get our first re-homed Newf. Our breeder, Nina, was ready to retire one of her top breeding girls by the name of Enchantee. Enchantee was a very large female, weighing about 160 pounds, and had produced many fine pups from two litters. She also was a very gentle, sweet Newf whom we had grown to know quite well during the times we had been helping Nina with her kennel. We debated for a very short time before agreeing that we could not let this offer go by. We became a three-dog household once again. Enchantee, like most other kennel dogs, took very quickly to being a house dog. She immediately fit in perfectly with our growing group.

After Kelsey left us, Murphy assumed the role of top dog in our household; however, Enchantee's first duty when she came to us was to change that situation. She arrived in late November, and it was Christmas Eve when she and Murphy had their first (and only) discussion about who was boss. Santa had given little toy hamburgers to all of the dogs for Christmas, and after receiving their respective toys each dog had retired to his or her own little area to chew or do whatever with them. At one point Murphy had left his toy and was innocently walking to the kitchen, perhaps to get some water. But he had to pass by Enchantee, who was still busy with her item. She assumed Murph was on his way to take the toy from her, so she promptly and very vocally chased him around the house and ended up nipping him on his nose. Murphy (the former boss) had run up onto the chesterfield to try to escape. From that day forward, Enchantee very quietly but confidently had Murph's attention.

Enchantee had asserted herself over Murphy, but with Bailey it was completely different. She and Bailey bonded very closely and very quickly. They would follow each other around all the time and lie together constantly. They became true friends. We enjoyed seeing this, especially because ever since Bailey had come to us it was either Kelsey ignoring him or Murphy dominating him. This was a refreshing change for the big boy.

Enchantee and Bailey

Enchantee napping on the futon

Each dog has unique characteristics that distinguish them as individuals. Murphy had a classy, sometimes aloof way about him, and Bailey had his food and a penchant for always sticking as close to me as physically possible. Enchantee's passion was her collection of Ingrid's and my possessions. She would wander through the house, gathering up shoes, socks, boots, underwear—anything she could find that belonged to Ingrid or me. If we were ever missing a glove, shoe, etc., we would automatically check Enchantee's private hiding place, which was usually in a corner of the living room. She quickly became known as the "Collector" Newf.

Peace and happiness reigned supreme in our little group for the next eighteen months. Then, suddenly, in February Enchantee became very sick, and we had to say goodbye to her. She was only six years old, and this was unexpected, so it was a very difficult time for the whole group. We were back to a two-Newf household. It may be difficult to understand, but even though we had three large dogs in the house for a year and a half, when we lost one, the house still managed to seem empty.

Sadly, even the two-Newf household did not last long. Bailey had been having some back problems for about one year, and it had progressed to the point where he had to be physically helped into the van whenever we went anywhere. The June following Enchantee's loss, Bailey had reached the point where we again had to make that difficult decision. We said goodbye to him while he rested in one of his favourite spots under a large maple tree at the back of the property. This was particularly difficult because we had never forgotten the terrible condition he was in five years earlier when we had taken him from the shelter, and he had shown his appreciation to us by becoming our first "Velcro" Newf—one who never left my side, no matter where I was or what I was doing. Even when I was doing some renovations in the house, with tools and materials all over the floor, the other dogs would be watching from a distance, but Bailey would lie right in the midst of it all, with his nose stuck right in there watching what I was doing. He was both my best buddy and my work supervisor all in one.

At the back end of the deck there were stairs of five steep steps leading down to the grass at the back of the house. He was having more and more difficulty using these steps, so we decided to build a ramp for him to make it easier. Fellow Newf owner and friend Lars had had senior Newfs in the past, so he know exactly what we were going through with this big boy. So one weekend we went out and purchased all the necessary material to construct this four-feet-wide and twelve-feet-long ramp. I spent about $500 on materials, Lars came over, and together we worked for two days to complete this project. Bailey died just before we finished construction. He never got to experience the joy of not having to struggle up those five steep steps.

We completed the ramp and hung a large wooden sign on the side of it that is still there today. It reads "The Bailey Steps."

Once again we were a one-Newf household. But not for long.

murphy, Bailey Enchantee and their humans

OuR CuRRent "Gaggle" of Newfs

This next section introduces the reader to our current gaggle of Newfs. Molly, Seven, Rimshot and Annie will be presented along with the story of how each one came to be with us and their individual characters and personalities. It will include a chronicling of many of the highlights of the latest few years of our life among the giants.

Molly of the Blue-Everyone's "Buddy"

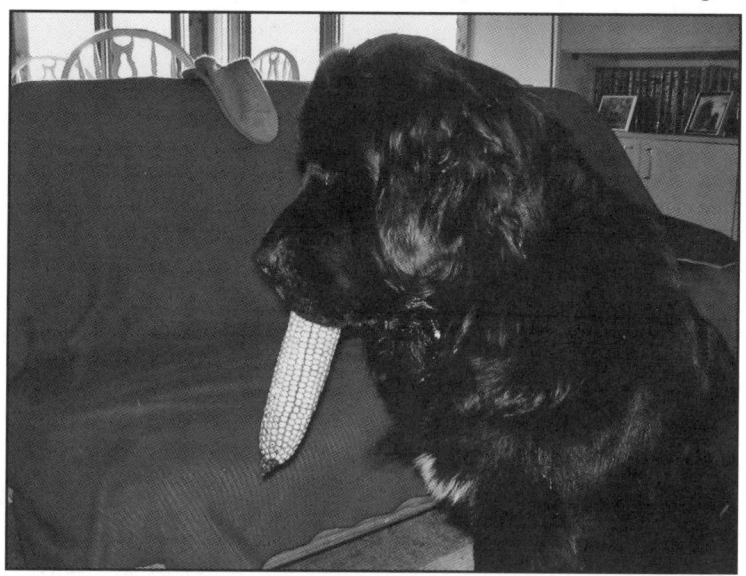

Bailey was our first rescue newf, so losing him was very difficult, and Nina must have known how it affected us because shortly thereafter she offered us a pup from her latest litter—one that she had planned on using in her breeding program. The only condition was that she could have one litter from her, and we immediately agreed. Since rescuing Bailey from the shelter years before, we had decided that any other dogs coming into our home would be rescues or re-homes. However, we accepted Nina's offer because this litter was from two of our favourite Marcarpents' dogs, Maneen and Rainbows End (Goldie). We knew (and still know) these two dogs very well and love the personality and character of both. So three-month-old Molly of the Blue came to live with us. She fit in right away, and

Murphy accepted her immediately. We feel that Murphy was probably a little intimidated by having another one of those "females" coming in to dominate him, so he never gave her any lip.

Murphy was now nine years old, and he was the last dog that we had had as a puppy. Bailey and Enchantee were both adult dogs at the time they joined our group. Now, here we were once again with a young, bouncy three-month-old puppy dog (who just happened to weigh about fifty pounds), and Molly very quickly reintroduced us to what it was like having a youngster around. One day, when we had been in the back part of the house for only a few minutes, we came out to the living room to an amazing sight. Ms. Molly had been in the bathroom and had grabbed one end of the toilet paper roll, running around the dining and living room with it still in her mouth. It looked as if the interior of our house had been toilet-papered by some mischievous Halloween pranksters. We were greeted by the sight of not only wall-to-wall toilet paper but also Molly sitting in the midst of this mess with toilet paper still draped across her face and head. And as usual, the "proper" Murphy was sitting away from the action, looking as innocent as possible.

molly and the saga of the toilet paper

Molly proved to be not only a typical young naughty dog but also a very intelligent one. This became apparent when we were walking in the fields one day shortly after her arrival. The dogs were off leash in the field, and as we neared the road we would call them to us to be leashed or at least under control. Molly was far out in front, and I called her, fully expecting to have to go to her instead of the other way around. Instead, she instantly turned and ran back. We had done no official training to that point, so this was a surprise. I then used the word *heel* and guided her to the spot simply by touching her collar. She fell into the heel position naturally and since that day has heeled on command like a pro. The same reaction came on the recall. When she is called or hears the whistle, she instantly turns from whatever she is doing and runs back to us. This happens consistently, regardless of the activity at the time. We have never had a dog that needed so little formal training to perform the basic commands. To this day, we are still occasionally surprised at how quickly she responds to a command. It is as if she wants to do anything she can to please us.

As mentioned earlier, one of the main reasons we accepted Molly was her parentage. Both of her parents are very social, friendly and beautiful Newfs, and Molly has followed in their genetic footsteps. She is one of the most social, kind and friendly dogs we have ever had. She always seems to want to please someone, be it human or dog. If a dog shows any impatience with her or, heaven forbid, growls at her, her reaction most often is to approach and lick. It's as if she is saying "Please don't be angry."

Classy molly-only bottled water for her

Her gentleness was shown when she was about one and a half years old. She and one of the other dogs were chasing a red squirrel around the back yard. She managed to corner the little critter, and before I could get there to rescue it, she had it in her mouth. My initial efforts to get to her to release it were futile as she seemed determined that this little guy was her new plaything. Finally, after a bit of running around, I caught up with her and with my arms around her neck firmly gave the command to "leave it." She then lowered her head to the ground and opened her mouth. Out popped "Lucky," who skittered away up a nearby tree. As it turned out, during the several minutes she had this guy in her mouth, she was actually cradling him in there amongst those large teeth but had held him with enough gentleness so as to do him no harm whatsoever.

During that first year, Molly and Murphy became great friends. Murphy was the senior and dominant one of the pair, and it seemed to us that he had taken on the role of showing Molly all the "things" they could do and enjoy. She followed him everywhere and took her lead directly from him.

murphy and molly ready for a ride

About one year after welcoming Molly, we had to say goodbye to Murphy. He was our first Newf and because of that was a special family member. It was again a difficult decision but made easier by the fact that he had had some problems with his back legs, and it had progressed to the point where we had to do something. He had enjoyed a good life with humans who cared for him and spoiled him too much. Back to a one-Newf household.

Originally, Molly was co-owned by us and Nina, and, as mentioned earlier, the agreement was that we would let Molly have one litter at the appropriate time. When that time came, we took her to Nina's for breeding with a beautiful Landseer boy by the name of the Rowdyman. The breeding took, and it wasn't long before we were taking her to Nina's for the birth of her litter.

Even though we had assisted with several litters in the past, Ingrid and I were quite stressed for this one. This was *our girl,* so it was very different from other litters. However, the event went smoothly, and Molly handled it well. We were quite relieved and very happy.

She had a litter of three beautiful, healthy pups, two black males and one Landseer girl. She turned out to be a great mother, which resulted in this being one of the easiest litters to raise. We lived a mere five miles from Nina at the time, so we spent every available hour over there with the mom and her pups. Molly very quickly made herself at home at the kennel but welcomed us enthusiastically each time we arrived. When we would leave to go home, she very gladly stayed with her new family. Eight weeks later her pups were placed, one in Toronto, Ontario, and two in the United States.

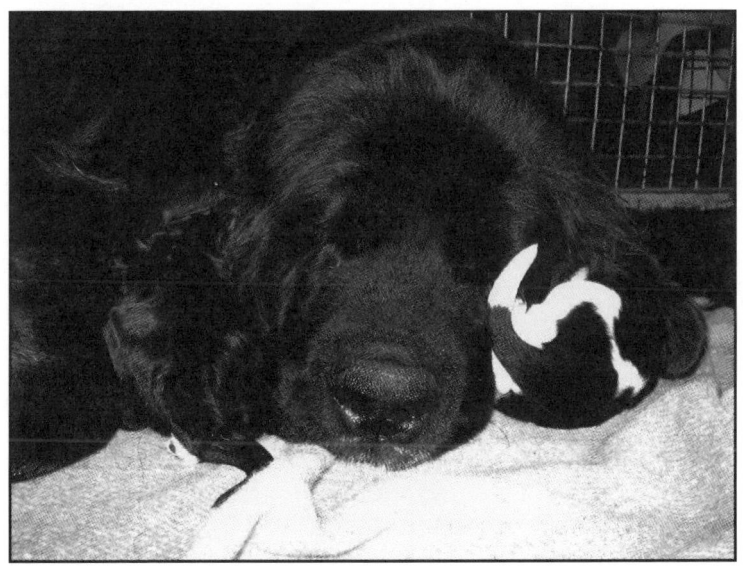

molly with two of her pups

"Divining" miss molly

Seven of nine—our latest "Velcro newf"

During these times, while we were enjoying our own Newfs, we were also helping Nina with her dogs at Marcarpents Kennels. We would look after her Newfs when she and hubby, Marc, went on holiday or at other times when we were needed. This was a real pleasure for us in many ways. One way was that we were always able to be near Newfoundland dogs. Another way was that we were learning so much from Nina about all aspects of the breed. During these times we became very close to her dogs. At that time she had twelve to fifteen in her kennel, and we knew the personality and character of each one of them. There was Seven of Nine, who was so named because she was the seventh girl in a litter of nine pups. She quickly became one of my favourites. Seven had this unique talent of being able to unlock the kennel gates and let other dogs out. Obviously, this is not a desirable trait for a dog in a breeding kennel. All of the dogs were let out of the kennels every day for exercise, but Seven did not enjoy this freedom as often as the others, simply because of her "gate-opening abilities." Sometimes when dogs were out running around I would catch a glimpse of Seven alone in one of the pens, watching…always gave a little "tug" in my heart to see that. Thus, when the time came for Seven to be retired from the breeding program and re-homed, we once again spent time (a very short time) considering bringing "one more dog" into our home. The thought of being able to give Seven a comfortable indoor life was just too tempting. She very happily joined our expanding group and became quite comfortable, thank you, as a "house" dog, and it took her about three minutes to do that. She is very large for a female Newf, weighing about 160 pounds, but is also one of the gentlest of dogs. Within a few days of "coming home" she happened upon a tiny baby rabbit in the backyard. Ingrid picked it up and carried it back to a chair on the deck. As she was holding it in her lap, Seven stood there with her huge muzzle tucked in under the tiny animal as if it were her baby. This was only a few days since she had left her litter at the kennel, so we assumed she was still in "mother mode."

One quality of this girl that became apparent right from the start was that she was very much like Bailey in that she could easily be labelled as one of those "Velcro" Newfs. She never left my side. No matter what I was doing or where I was doing it—there was Seven of

Nine, sticking her nose in and attempting to be as close as possible to the action.

Sometimes it seems as though Seven has never lost those motherly qualities. Whenever someone coughs or sneezes, and I mean almost *every* time, Seven comes from wherever she is and from whatever she is doing to go to the person in question to make sure everything is okay. She will stare at the "patient" for a minute, receive a reassuring hug and then go back to whatever she was doing.

She is the least dominant dog we have ever had the pleasure of owning. For a while, we had to intervene at dinner time to teach Molly not to finish her dinner and then head to Seven's dish to finish hers. As Molly would approach, Seven would just stop eating and back up so Molly would have easy access to her dinner. It took us a very short while to straighten that out.

Seven reminds us of Pig Pen, the character from the Peanuts cartoons. We can spend an hour grooming this girl so that she is looking great. But ten minutes later, she looks as if we hadn't groomed her in months. During the summer, dirt and debris seem to follow her wherever she goes.

molly checking out new friend, Seven

Seven making sure no crumbs fall

Rimshot, the "boss," arrives

One of the top dogs in nina's kennel was a boy named Rimshot. In his younger years he weighed 180 to 190 pounds. He is a massive-boned guy with a personality that matches his physical appearance. He was top dog in the kennel, and he carried himself in a very appropriate, confident manner. Rimshot earned his championship at the ripe young age of eighteen months, which speaks loudly about the quality of this big guy.

In October 2000, the Dicken Award, commonly described as the "animal Victoria Cross," was presented posthumously to a Newfoundland dog named Gander. Gander was a mascot for some Canadian soldiers fighting in Hong Kong during the Second World War. He gave his life to save these soldiers by running away with a thrown grenade and dying in the explosion. The presentation ceremony took place at the home of the British high commissioner in Ottawa, and in attendance along with other dignitaries was veteran Frederick Kelley. Mr. Kelly was one of Gander's handlers during the war.

Rimshot was lucky enough to be chosen to represent Gander at the ceremony and to receive the award in his stead. He was an excellent representative of the breed, and when Mr. Kelley saw him, memories flooded back and he was quite overcome. It was an emotional moment for all.

During the years we were helping Nina and Marc care for their dogs, Rimshot never ceased to amaze me in the way he exuded quiet control over himself and his kennelmates. He never seemed to become excited unless he was in "play mode." During the times we were babysitting the kennel, one of the many pleasurable duties was to let the dogs out for a run a couple of times during the day. When the other dogs were let out, it was a "run around and chase someone" time, but Rimshot was different. When he was let out he walked around very calmly, as if surveying the property to make sure all was well. His routine was to stroll up the hill to the woods at the back of the property, do his "business" on top of the first tree stump in the woods, then walk back to the pens. I would always make that walk with him.

One day Rim and I were strolling back to the pens when John, the neighbour from down the road, walked up to talk. As he approached Rimshot, who was by my side, Rim emitted a low growl. This took me by surprise because I had never heard him do that. When one hears a noise like that emitting from a 180-pound dog, one takes notice. But John was prepared and had some treats ready for him. However, before he could even offer the treats, Rim rushed forward, grabbed John's hat from his hands and ran away. He ran circles around us, leaping in the air with this hat dangling from his mouth, running up close and then taking off again, obviously teasing the owner of that hat. It was great seeing this huge dog bouncing around like a little puppy, but I never did understand the growl. We just assumed it was his way of warning John to hold on to his hat!

Nina also has a special place in her heart for Rimshot, and I don't think she would ever have placed him in a home had we not been available and willing. We lived quite close to the kennel, and she knew of our love for the breed and for Rim. So when he turned nine years of age, she made us an offer of letting us take this aging guy from the outdoor environment and give him the comforts of an indoor life. Well, how could we ever turn down an offer like that? We considered it an honour to have this dog living with us, and will be eternally grateful to Nina for giving us this opportunity. So here we were, back to a three-Newf household.

Rim has been with us for over two years, and as he has settled in as an indoor dog, his personality and character have blossomed. He started immediately to assume his role as top dog in the house. Molly and Seven accepted this as the most natural situation they could imagine. They have never once challenged him. Seven, Rimshot's daughter, most likely remembered him from her kennel days and just reasoned that this is the way it is supposed to be. Molly would never challenge anyone, no matter who it was, so this was an easy transition.

We have found it most interesting to watch how the pack, including Ingrid and I, changes when a dominant male comes into the house. Rim considers me as alpha male in the pack and himself as second in command. Every evening, while we are sitting around the house, Rimshot will go to one of the back bedrooms to sleep, leaving me in charge of all the "subordinates." If I leave the girls and join him in the other part of the house, he will immediately move to take his position back with the ladies. If I keep moving back and forth from one area to the other, he will do the same, only in reverse. Before we understood his reasons, this was quite puzzling; however, we now understand that he is fulfilling his role as one of the dominant members of the pack.

When we go for walks with the whole group (today, four Newfs, Ingrid and me), Rim is always checking to make sure all is well with the pack and everyone is where they should be. The other dogs are more concerned with looking and sniffing, but Rim always seems to be glancing over his shoulder to make sure no one is left behind.

Dominant though he may be, he still shows a little insecurity when we go out and leave him home. One of the first things we have to do when we return home is to head to the bay window in the dining room to gather all the items that Rim has put there while we were away. The window looks out on the driveway at the front of the house, and he spends his time making trip after trip from our bedroom at the back of the house to the bay window at the front to deposit his items. When we arrive home we find all types of clothing, from jeans, sweaters and jackets to shoes and boots, all piled on the shelf of the window. He will pick up anything left on the bed or chairs in the bedroom but will also stick his head into the closet to pull out other items that he deems necessary for his collection.

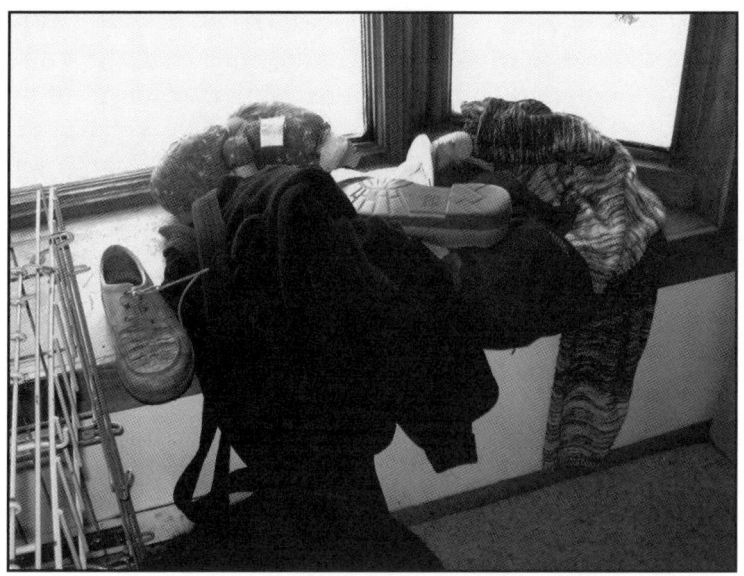

Rimshot's "Collection"

In 2005, the Canadian Newfoundland Specialty was held in Gananoque, Ontario. We decided to give Rimshot one last experience in the show ring and registered him in the veteran's class, parade of champions and parade of veterans. This was a new experience for Ingrid and me. We had been to many dog shows, but this was the first time in the ring for both of us. The show is held outdoors, and on that day the weather was perfect. Everything went well in the ring. Rim placed second in the veteran's class, and Ingrid and I performed admirably in the ring for the two parade events. Breeders, handlers and dogs come from all over Canada and the United States and some from Europe for this show, and it amazed me at how quickly word spread around the grounds that Rimshot was in attendance. While in the ring with him, I could hear many comments from spectators, mentioning his name. He is a special Newf, and this was an exciting day for all of us.

Rim in the ring for his last show with marc Cote (2005)

Rimshot out for a walk with his ever-present stuffed toy

Because of his age, now eleven, we must shorten Rim's walks. He tires quickly, so we are pampering him a little more than usual. When we walk in the fields in the winter, we follow a snowmobile trail of packed snow. On a recent such excursion I had all four dogs out in the woods for some exercise and some sniffing around (the dogs do the sniffing). At one point the girls took off through the woods following moose or deer tracks, and Rimshot tried his best to keep up. They charged down one side of a huge gully—about ten feet deep and filled with snow—and charged up the other side. However, Rimshot, when he made it to the bottom of the gully, just stopped and stood there, because he could not get up the other side and also could not get back up the way he had gone down. Being a hero, I climbed down into the ditch and pulled and pushed him back to the top. Everything went okay, but this was not a pretty sight. The snow at the bottom of the ditch was at least three feet deep, and it was difficult to maintain footing. At one point I was lying on my stomach on the side of the hill with my hands pushing his bum from behind, and when I looked to the top I could see the girls sitting up there side by side, watching my struggle. It would have been quite comical had I not had several pounds of snow jammed down the inside of my coat and boots.

The closeness of the group was again demonstrated when I finally got him to the top. The others seemed to be very relieved and were all over him, welcoming him back to the fold.

wilderness treks

OUR CURRENT "GAGGLE" OF NEWFS

L'il Orphan Annie—Full-Speed Annie

A few years ago while we were visiting with Nina at the kennel, I was present at the birth of a litter of twelve pups. The mother of this litter was a small (120-pound) girl named L'il Orphan Annie. I remember thinking at the time that this was a beautiful Newf, smaller than most, but seemingly perfectly proportioned and with an absolutely beautiful coat and wonderful gentle personality. Shortly after having this litter, she was re-homed to a family who also lived in this area. She was with them for less than a year when the caregiver of that family suffered a serious accident and had to spend several weeks in the hospital and several months recuperating at home. We offered to take Annie in temporarily until the owner was once again able to care for the dog. Time passed, and the owner's situation was improving, but very slowly. By this time Annie had spent more time with us than she had with her new family originally. So we mutually agreed that for Annie's benefit she would stay with us permanently

Annie has a personality much like Seven of Nine. She is very soft and gentle, and the two seem to be fighting to see who can occupy the bottom rung of the ladder in the hierarchy of the pack. And they both win. They are no one's boss, and they love it that way. Annie, being a smaller Newf, has more energy than the larger dogs. She is faster, bouncier and has more staying power when playing. And everywhere she goes, she runs (hence the nickname Full Speed Annie). Where toys are involved, she is not shy to grab something from out of the mouths of one of the other dogs. That was fine right up until the time she tried it with Rimshot. This was her first lesson that she was not the boss in this house. He chased her around the backyard, leaving her sitting at the back fence wondering what had just happened. I don't think she completely understood the meaning of that lesson, because it took her many months to get up the courage to play like that again with Molly and Seven, but she never did try it again with Rim.

Annie, like most Newfs, loves to be around her humans, but she loves being with other dogs as well. She is uncomfortable taking walks when the other three are left at home. If we take her to the fields without other dogs, she enjoys the time but never strays far from us, walking calmly by our side. However, when the other dogs are with us, she is a fireball of energy, charging here and there.

By now our group has settled into a very comfortable routine. We have three dogs of 160 to 170 pounds each, plus one of 120 pounds. There is never a disagreement among them, and we seldom have to deal with a behaviour problem. We do, however, have to take certain measures when we go out and leave Seven home. We have rabbits all around the house, and if she spots one outside the window, any potted plants left on or near the windowsill will be destined for the floor. We have therefore changed some things to accommodate this little inconvenience. Every time we go out and leave Seven at home, blinds are pulled down, curtains are drawn and coffee table and chairs are set up to block access to windows.

annie and Seven under the deck, escaping the sun

Seven of nine back from a winter walk

annie and molly

annie, feeling no stress

FITTING FOUR NEWFS INTO TWENTY-FOUR HOURS

Obviously, living with four Newfoundland dogs in the house is a challenge. However, we tend to most often adjust our lifestyle and habits to "please" the dogs. This section should give the reader a good indication of the sacrifices we gladly endure in order to live among the giants.

The "Pack"

These four dogs have grown exceptionally close to each other. We still are not accustomed to the fact that mealtime with four large dogs is so organized. Each has his or her regular place to eat, all within five to ten feet of each other. Molly usually finishes first and then stands behind Seven, waiting to lick her empty dish. She then proceeds to stand behind Rim, and then Annie. After all of the dishes have been licked clean by all four dogs, they all proceed down the ramp to the back of the house for the after-meal business, the three girls first in line and Rimshot bringing up the rear, waiting to pee on every spot that the girls have visited, just to reinforce the fact that he is still king here.

When we take one or two dogs with us somewhere and leave the others at home, the scene upon returning is one as if we had been gone for days. The girls especially go from dog to dog, many licks and bouncing around, acting like everyone is quite relieved that the group is finally back together.

A couple of days ago I took the four of them for a walk up our street. When I take the four of them alone, I put the troublemakers, Seven and Annie, on leash, and Molly and Rim usually walk off leash. That day Rim did not feel like going and stood at the end of the driveway watching the rest of us walk away. I kept walking and looking back to see if he was coming, but he stood like a statue, just watching. The girls were obviously not comfortable seeing him that far back and not with the group. Eventually I was halfway up the street, which was a good two city blocks from him. When I decided to

81

go back and put him in the house, Molly suddenly took off for home full speed until she reached him and then proceeded to cover him with kisses, bouncing around him. The "staid" Rimshot just stood there, soaking it all in...I just love watching these dogs relate to each other

This close bond exists not only in our immediate group. Our grandson, Tyler, who is six years old, has grown up with our dogs. When he was just starting to get around on hands and knees, it was Bailey who adopted him and would follow him everywhere. He seemed to take on the role of protector when Tyler was visiting. As anyone who owns Newfs knows, people often ask, "How can you tell them apart?" Tyler not only knows who is who with our dogs but he knows the personality traits of all four of them. He will sit on the floor with them, often for no other reason than just to be near them. All four dogs treat him as a member of the pack and, surprisingly, as one of the leaders of the pack. Some of the nicest moments with Tyler and the dogs were when he was bonding with Rimshot. Tyler was four years old, and Rim had been with us only a short time. They both seemed to gravitate to each other for companionship, and the memories of this little guy sharing moments with the then 170-pound Rimshot and the others are priceless.

Tyler, molly and annie

molly looking for leftovers

Best buddy Rimshot

molly

Starting the Day with Newf Hair in the Butter

Of course there are breeds other than Newfs that shed their coat, but Newf hair is special. It is black and fine, and it floats. It gently floats around the house, coming to rest in some of the most unusual and surprising and sometimes embarrassing places.

There is nothing like getting up in the morning and jumping into a hot shower to start the day. Then when you're finished, grabbing a fresh towel off the rack and burying your dripping wet face into that freshly laundered piece of 100 percent cotton. But wait! This cannot be 100 percent cotton. At least 10 percent of this towel is Newf hair, and most of that 10 percent is now stuck in your eyes, your nose and half into your mouth. But, you think to yourself, "Didn't this towel just come from the laundry this morning?" Yes, it did, and this is part of life among the giants.

Then, after picking all that hair off your body, piece by piece, you head for the kitchen to prepare breakfast. Toast and eggs sound good? You bet! You crack that egg into the frying pan, and there, actually imbedded in and deeply contrasted against the bright yellow yolk, is another solid black strand of hair. Now try to pick it out without breaking that delicate yolk. Up pops the toast, and you reach for the margarine. Upon opening the container, there is another one of those long black souvenirs clinging to the inside of the container top. This is also part of life among the giants.

This same routine is repeated as you remove a cup from the cupboard for your morning coffee and a plate for your toast and eggs. The most amazing aspect of all is that when we notice these anomalies—we don't even give them a second thought. We don't get angry or frustrated. We don't discuss moving these animals out of the house to a kennel. We don't quickly grab the vacuum and rush madly around the house. We just simply don't care! One might say that when we shop, we buy items like Newf yogurt, Newf cheese, Newf eggs, Newf margarine, etc. This is part of accepting life among the giants.

This attitude is shared with almost every other Newf owner who may be visiting, be it for dinner or simply for coffee. In these instances of a found treasure, one may hear comments such as "Ugh, a Newf hair!," after which there is a burst of laughter from the group. However, most likely no one will mention it, because they have become so accustomed to it that hair just disappears along with that bite of biscuit or sip of coffee. Newf owners generally regard this as an additional source of protein or fibre. Newf hair at the table is so common that often someone will comment if they *haven't* found one.

Newf owners love to share stories about where one finds that lost Newf hair. Some of the more interesting places are (courtesy of Lars Erup)

- Wrapped around a lipstick
- Wound around the bristles of a toothbrush (which is kept in a closed drawer)
- As texture on a painting
- Behind a computer monitor glass
- Inside a baked potato
- In worn pantyhose

- In a jar of Nivea face cream (only after it has been applied)

Of course this nonchalance disappears when we are expecting guests for dinner who are non-Newf-aware people. Then pandemonium reigns. It's a mad race around the house with a magnifying glass, seeking out each tiny Newf hair and dispatching it to the special Newf-hair garbage bag, which is always hanging on a doorknob in the porch. Every dish and utensil now gets the once-over with that same magnifying glass. Perhaps the most radical procedure in preparation for non-Newf guests is that we will bring out a brand new, never-been-used set of towels and facecloths from a back room. These are purchased months in advance and are kept sealed in a back room, well away from the source of these ubiquitous black hairs, just for times like these.

We really do enjoy having guests who are not accustomed to having four Newfs around the house. In these cases, the conversation often centres on the dogs. We find it especially entertaining after the meal to watch the expressions on their faces as we line up the four dogs in the kitchen and let them clean the plates. However, the real entertainment starts when they notice that the plates nonchalantly go directly from the Newfs to the cupboard.

Sitting in the kitchen waiting for the "Plate Lick"

Pardon me while I wipe That Slime off the Ceiling

Some newfs drool. Some newfs drool more than others. Some Newfs drool quarts. With four Newfs in the house, vacuuming and wiping up the Newf hair is only part of it. There is a continuous discussion on Internet Newf lists and among Newf folks in general as to what is the best product on the market for cleaning slime off the refrigerator, cupboard doors, etc. Everyone has their favourite solution, be it commercial or one handed down by Newf owners of the past.

One would expect to have to clean the bottom part of the refrigerator or the bottom three feet of the walls, but one would *not* expect to have to have a small stepladder always handy so one could reach those streaks of slime at the junction of the top of the wall and the ceiling. And what does one use to get slime off a stucco ceiling? Who knows! Spit happens! No area of the house is safe from a Newf who has just had half of his twenty-pound head immersed in a water dish, sucking up his water, then stood back up and had a good shake. We have trained our ears so that when a dog drinks, we know it. We then are ready with one of our many "drool rags" to catch that spray before the shake. Rimshot, before he became old and lazy, adapted to the routine and would have a drink and then immediately come to one of us for the "wipe off." Now he just doesn't seem to care. He will have a drink and then walk away from the water dish, trailing a river flowing from his chin and chest. Love those old guys. We keep drool rags scattered in different areas of the house so that we are never too far from one.

Also, whenever we take these dogs anywhere where there may be other people, a drool rag is stuffed into a back pocket, ready to be whipped out at a moment's notice.

There is never a thought given to throwing away an old towel. Everything is considered a potential drool rag. Yes, this is life among the giants.

molly asks Rimshot, "Could you please clean that from under my chin?"

Just a Little Off the Top, Please

In case anyone is curious, yes, grooming is important. Grooming is critical when you have Newfs! Lack of grooming can be a disaster. This is especially true if your Newfs have the privilege of running free in fields and wooded areas, as ours do. These dogs have an affinity for seeking out the mud puddles and burdocks wherever they are. Newfoundlands have long silky double coats, which are beautiful when well groomed, but four of them with imbedded dirt, grass and burdocks can mean you will not enjoy a relaxing evening in front of the TV tonight, and maybe not for a few nights. The well equipped Newf owner has many dollars invested in several types of grooming utensils. We have our de-matter, for those stubborn knots down close to the skin. Most of us have several different types of these. Then we have our rakes for the outer coat (again, many different styles). We have thinning scissors, regular scissors, nail clippers (the large size, of course) and a couple of metal combs (also the large ones). Then we have many different sprays, conditioners, and the all-important gallon of dog shampoo, which, if you're lucky, will do all four Newfs. Some of us have one of those dryers that are powerful enough to blow away a small child but are barely adequate to dry a Newf.

In the summer, our grooming sessions take place up on an old picnic table. Rimshot is the exception. Because of his age we don't ask him to climb up there any more; rather, we get down on our hands and knees to be at his level to get it done. It's not important that the arthritis in my knees is worse than his. However, during the winter we do not groom outside in minus-thirty degrees C. Now we groom in the living room. The amount of coat that comes out of a Newf in one grooming would shock many non-Newf folks. Our friend Lars measures this amount as "removing so many poodles from our dog." We can easily accumulate one large plastic garbage bagful of coat in one four-Newf session.

molly with her barber(ette)

Seven waiting her turn

Furnishing a Four-newf Household

many sacrifices have to be made in order to have a four-Newf household. One of them is the furniture we purchase. Comforters for the bed are never of a light colour, and heaven forbid that we should have a white duvet. Everything is coloured so that black does not show well. Living room furniture recently has come out in great new fabrics like Microsoft Velour. So attractive and comfortable. We don't have that! We have a functional, durable chesterfield, many colours but predominately darker colours. How many families have a double-sized futon mattress on the living room floor exclusively to be used as a dog's bed? Our living room floor is covered with dog blankets. and the arms of chairs and chesterfields have drool rags draped over them. This is another reason that we *never* throw away a towel, no matter what its condition. Most of our floors are wall to wall carpeting, and when we installed it, what were we thinking? We actually chose a light grey for the colour. Well, five years later, this is no longer a light grey. I could not describe the colour, but suffice it to say that we will be replacing that carpeting this year with a colour more appropriate for a four-Newf household.

Rim keeping an eye on his flock (sort of)

Sometimes we ask, "Who actually is in charge here?"

Gotta keep each other warm at night

Regarding clothing: Our closets are filled with blue denim and dark-coloured T-shirts and sweaters. Our bright summer colours are dark blue, dark green and dark white. When we do dress up to go out (without the dogs), we wait until the very last minute before putting on our "non-Newf clothes." Then, once we are dressed, it is a constant battle to stay away from the dogs until safely out the door. A clothes brush is a staple for us, and it is critical to have a partner to give you that final once-over for those slime marks and Newf hair once you are in the car.

Our Daily Routine—The "n" in Newf Is not for "normal"

This morning, while I have been sitting at the computer, working on this book, Rimshot and Molly have been lying outside in the sun. Rim just barked to come in, and when I opened the door this guy (eleven years old) charged through the door to the box where we have all the stuffed toys, grabbed a couple of them in his mouth, and is now running all around the house, room to room, barking a muffled bark while holding these two stuffed animals in his mouth. I was going to take Molly to therapy today, but I think, with all this energy, this fellow should be there. So good to see him like this!

Most people rely on their alarm clock to wake up each morning and then have to fight the snooze button to actually get out of bed. In our house we have no need for such devices. We have the four-legged variety of alarm clocks, and we have four of those. The "waking up" routine usually starts around seven each morning, when I wake up to a presence on the bed. It is most often a heavy weight on my legs, which if left unattended would most certainly cut off all blood supply to my feet. This would be Annie, curled up at the foot of the bed but with the front part of her body draped over my legs. At the same time I feel this hot, moist breath on my face, and upon opening my eyes, I find myself inches away from a large panting beast. This would be Seven, lying at the head of the bed with her head on the pillow, staring at me, waiting for me to wake up.

Now the secret is to remain as calm as possible until I am ready to extricate myself from these two. If I give any indication that I am awake, then I am shocked by Molly rushing to the bedside and burying her head under the blankets and enthusiastically licking everything within reach. This would be followed by Rimshot, either excitedly barking from the living room telling me to get up or charging into the bedroom and also burying his head (and cold nose) into my back. Rarely do I slowly and pleasantly wake up to face the day.

Once I step out of bed, the challenge is to make it out of the bedroom without tripping over these milling giant dogs, who are more interested in head rubs and scratches than anything else. Following this excitement, I let them all outside to do the morning "business." They all go down the ramp that leads off the deck, in single file, Rimshot bringing up the rear. His role apparently is to follow each member of his harem and ensure that he pees in exactly the same spot that each one of them does. This keeps him busy for quite a while. Then they all meander back to the deck and collapse outside the patio door for their naps. Meanwhile, I am now wide awake and wondering just who actually is the "boss" in this house.

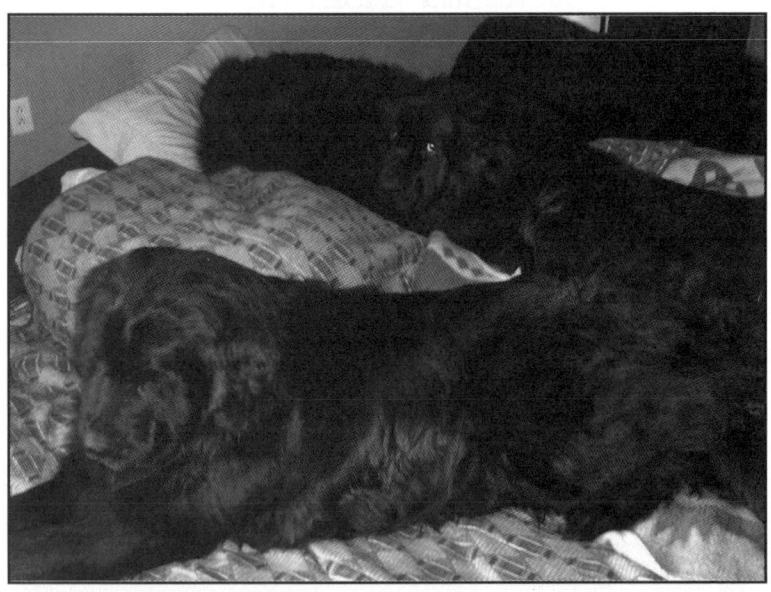

Somewhere there is a human trying to sleep

Only good dreams can come from this

The dogs spend most of the day intently watching every move I make as I move around the house. They are looking for the slightest indication that I am about to put on a jacket or boots. This action is immediately construed as confirmation that we are going out and results in pandemonium. So it is imperative that I watch my every move as I go about my daily activities.

We have one of those portable air conditioners in the living room and one more in the bedroom. These are a necessity with Newfs in the house. Often on a hot, humid summer day we will notice it becoming increasingly warm and humid in the living room. The reason is that we often have three of the four Newfs crowded around the cool air outlet, blocking it from the room.

When, in fact, I actually have to go somewhere, I take the four of them with me if at all possible. On the way home, most often we will stop at a wooded area close by and spend some time wandering the fields and woods. If I am unable to take them with me, then it is a major operation for me to get out the door without a dog. They have become used to the phrase "I'll be back in a minute," and when they hear that, they usually calm down because they know they are not going with me. They will lie around the door with that mournful look on their face that says they are the most ill-treated creatures in the world.

If they don't go with me in the car (actually, with four Newfs, that must read "van"), then I take them for walks during the day. I have tried a few times to take all four at once, but as one would imagine, that can be a disaster of tangled leashes and a frustrated human. So I will take two at a time. Now this can be a traumatic event for the two who are left behind. The way I choose who goes and who stays is generally by opening the patio door about two feet, and whichever two of the four get out first are the ones who get to go. If I look back to the house as I am walking away, there are always two big black heads silhouetted in the dining room window, watching every step I take. When I return twenty to thirty minutes later, these same two heads are still there waiting. This process is reversed when I switch to take the other two.

The day progresses with one of the four barking to go out every twenty to thirty minutes. Then, of course, each one has to come back in again. Trying to sit quietly and read a book for a while is virtually impossible. In the summer or on the more pleasant winter days, three of the four spend most of the time outside. Seven is the exception. She loves being inside, lying in front of the fire, as cozy as possible. Also, being our current "Velcro" Newf, she always wants to be wherever I am.

We find that we really do not have to have clocks or watches around the house to know when it is 3:45 p.m. Fifteen minutes before dog dinner time— wherever we are, whatever we are doing—we will be suddenly surrounded by four panting, pacing Newfs, all looking for their dinner. After they have eaten and performed their after-dinner routine, the next "big event" of the day is Ingrid's arrival home from work. This important time is signalled by Molly, Seven and Annie gathering at the gate, sitting side by side and staring at the driveway. As each car comes around the bend in the road, three heads seem to stand up and take notice but settle down as the car passes by the house. This is repeated with every car that comes into sight until Ingrid turns into the driveway. Once again pandemonium ensues by welcoming the final family member safely back into the fold.

Our evenings are usually spent quietly with four huge bodies spread out on the floor like so many bearskin rugs. The only way we know that we have these four giants in the house is having to get up periodically to let one or more of them outside and then minutes later back inside. We are most thankful to have a TV remote and a satellite receiver that allows us to pause live TV. When living with four Newfoundland dogs in the house, these are essential tools. Typically, a two-hour movie takes about three hours to watch. We have become accustomed to the following: Five minutes after the start of the movie, a dog will bark at the door to go out. Pause. Back to the movie. Then another will notice that someone is outside and want to go out also. Pause. Back to the movie. A few minutes later Rimshot wanders out from his back-room nap and notices that two dogs are missing. Pause. Back to the movie. Next is for one of the outside dogs to bark to come in. Another pause. Back to the movie. This little routine is repeated many times during the "two" hour movie and is a normal occurrence. Add to this the many times one of the dogs will walk into the living room and stop and sit directly in front of the TV, completely obliterating the screen. Pause—wait until he or she moves on.

The bedtime routine is the same every night. The last trip outside is made about 11 p.m., followed by the nightly treat. This is Rimshot's cue to head for the back bedroom. When we make our appearance, followed by Seven, Annie and Molly, Rimshot immediately heads for the dining room, where he will spend the night. The three girls have their specific spots on the floor to sleep. One important fact that must be mentioned here is that most Newfs snore. And they snore loudly. Most could win snoring contests with the loudest human snorer. We have family and friends who can rattle the windows with their snoring but can still be outdone by a Newf. However, it is quite interesting that we find it almost impossible to sleep with a human snoring on the other side of the bedroom wall, but three or four Newfs shaking the floor is akin to having a glass of warm milk before bedtime.

waiting at the door for mom to come home

This is a crowded living room

Every ten-year-old deserves a birthday party

A crowded day at the beach

Everyone in his place at mealtime

Waiting at the gate for mom to come home

If I could only get them to pick up a shovel...

...or a rake!

molly and Ingrid

Looks like we have our "ducks in a row"

Sometimes Sixteen Feet Feels Like Sixteen Tons

Anyone in a multi-dog household (especially large dogs) will know that it is virtually impossible to have a nice, full and green lawn. All the traffic and peeing quickly creates these not-so-attractive areas where vegetation withers and fades away. As dutiful homeowners, each spring we order a load of topsoil and diligently spread, roll and seed these areas, trying our best to beat the inevitable. We put up temporary barriers to keep the dogs off, and often grass will grow, but just as often it quickly disappears as soon as the barriers are removed. So we have resigned ourselves to these areas being a necessary part of living with giants.

Apart from their less than desirable appearance, these bare spots take on another role on a rainy day. Areas with no grass become areas of mud, and dogs, whether it is raining or bright sunshine, must go outside to do their daily "eliminations." Our routine on these rainy days would leave many standing with their mouths open trying to figure out "just what is wrong with these people?" Newfs love water. Water comes in many forms—lakes, rivers, oceans and of course rain—so when they go outside to do their business, they usually are in no hurry to get back. They wander the property from muddy area to muddy area, looking for that perfect spot, then wander some more, investigating every little clump of grass (sparse though these may be). By the time they get back to the door, they are not a pretty sight—soaking wet, and mud halfway up their legs.

In order to cope with these days, we have adopted a routine. We cover our kitchen floor with many of the "dog" blankets we keep for these occasions, the dogs line up on the deck outside the door, and one by one they come in. They stand patiently while we towel off their coats, which now seems to weigh an additional ten pounds because of the water. Then we proceed from foot to foot with a wet towel, cleaning the mud from the feet, legs and between the toes. As each dog is completed, he or she is shuffled off to another room and the next one is brought in for the same treatment. This usually takes about fifteen minutes to complete, and on a typical rainy day we execute this routine three or four times.

Foot washing or washing of feet is a religious rite observed as an ordinance by several Christian denominations. Obviously the reason we practice this ritual is not one of religion. I must add that we do this only for the dogs. Human visitors must arrange their own foot cleaning.

Out and About with Newfs

A newfoundland is a type of dog that is not well known among non-Newf people. When a Newf owner is out and about with their dogs, a large part of that time is spent being stopped and questioned by people who are fascinated by the size, colour and "teddy bear" appearance of this giant. There are a series of questions all Newf owners are asked repeatedly:

"Do they eat a lot?"
"You don't keep that dog in the house, do you?"
"You must have a big house!"
"They must need a lot of exercise!"
"How much does he weigh?"
"Do you have a saddle for that horse?"
"You have *four* of them?"

And the most often asked question:

"What kind of dog is that?"

Many people think they know what kind of dog it is and will sometimes tell the owner what kind of dog he has. Newf owners are always comparing and sharing the stories about what their Newf has been called. Probably the two dogs most often confused with a Newf are the Bouvier and the Saint Bernard, both of which are nice dogs but look nothing like a Newf.

It is quite interesting, however, when some well-meaning people who just happen to know a little about dogs in general give their idea of what breed this is. Some of the names that they come up with are quite fascinating. Lars Erup, a long time Newf owner and good friend, has maintained a list of names that Newfs have been called. Some of the more imaginative are (with his permission),

Overweight Afghan
Cocker spaniel
Flat-coated retriever on steroids
Maltese
Pit bull (giant black)
Shih Tzu
Newfoundlander sheepdog (nonexistent breed)
St. New Finlander (nonexistent breed)
Black Angus calf
Burmese (that's a cat!)
Clydesdale (that's a horse)
Great Dane
Some sort of large poodle
Badly bred St. Bernard

Socializing with Friends and Their Newfs

The newfoundland dog world is a small and unique one, so Newf owners tend to develop relationships and friendships with one another. We have been very fortunate in that most of our group live within a reasonable travel time, so we get together regularly with our dogs. The scenes at these gatherings are quite remarkable. It is quite the sight to see six to eight Newfs (or more) plus their owners all having lunch and socializing on a deck on a summer day. Our fellow Newf owners, at least the ones in our immediate group, are all as fanatical about their dogs as we are. It is quite an interesting sight to see four or six humans sitting down to dinner to enjoy a nicely decorated table, a succulent roast beef or similar tasty meat, with nicely baked potatoes and fresh, colourful vegetables. Sprawled all over the kitchen floor and under the table you may find anywhere from two to six Newfs snoring away. It would seem as though they are all sound asleep, but you can be sure that they all have one eye on that table looking intently at those humans, just waiting for a sign that they have finished their meal. They know that when the meal is done, the plate licking begins. Now a bunch of humans letting these huge dogs clean off the plates (often two Newfs on the same plate) is a sight to behold but in fact is a common occurrence in our group.

Of course, owners of most breeds of dog enjoy this friendship and camaraderie, but because of the unique personality and the massive size of the Newf, this social aspect is a little different. Not only do we share the personality and character of our dogs, but, strange as it may seem, we are all very proud of the fact that our dogs are droolers and shedders. In fact, occasionally we brag about whose dog drools the most or who has the dog with the most unmanageable coat.

Newf owners are also a little different in that most of us eventually realize that one Newf is simply not enough. We may start out with the intention of having a dog, but it does not take long before we are expanding our families. After all, we must make good use of that central vacuum system. So you often will see families with three, four, five, and even more Newfs.

When we get together, either for formal events or casual get-togethers, somehow water is often involved. Newfs love water, and when you get them together at a lake or river, it usually turns into a water fest, with both dogs and owners frolicking like children at a swimming pool. A Newf's water rescue instincts can sometimes present unique problems. We know Newf owners who, when at a cottage on or near water, must first put the Newf into the house before taking the children for a swim. This is because the dog will not allow a child to go near or, heaven forbid, in the water. It makes it quite evident that in its opinion this is not a safe place and will constantly herd the child away from the water's edge.

In the past we have gathered for Newf picnics, Newf swims, Newf walks and even a Newf baseball game— this is when a group of Newf owners play a normal game of baseball but each player has a Newf on leash. The Newf must stay with the player throughout the game, from pitching to batting and running the bases. Of course the game is seldom taken seriously, and often during the game you can find one of the players in the outfield lying down on the grass wrestling with his Newf, oblivious to the baseballs falling all around them.

Another of the fun events we have had was an annual Newf picnic. One of the most memorable of these was one year when we had perhaps twenty adults and ten or twelve Newfs. We were gathered at a small park that was situated along the shores of the St. Lawrence and had a small beach. We had arranged several picnic tables so as to create one large eating area. These were always a pot luck arrangement where everyone brought one or two of their favourite dishes. This day we had all this food laid out on three or four tables and were set to settle down to eat when a sudden storm came roaring down the river. Within minutes the winds had whipped up to a point where we all witnessed birds flying backwards. The rain came down in torrents, soaking everything in sight. It all lasted a mere ten minutes and then was gone, but by then everything and everyone was thoroughly soaked. Amazingly, this failed to dampen our spirits, and we all had a great time and still talk about it today. It also goes without saying that the Newfs were in their glory during this downpour. All that water!

The next picnic we held in this park, the following year, was just as interesting. At some point between the two events, the owners of the park had changed the rules to limit use of the park to the residents of the immediate area (and none of us fit into that category).

So at the next picnic, in our ignorance, we set up everything as we had done in the past, tables together and all the food laid out. It was a beautiful sight, all those colourful dishes, people and Newfs all smiling and anticipating a day of fun. Then just as we were settling down to eat, the manager of the facilities showed up to inform us that we were not supposed to be there and we would have to leave immediately. Our pleas to let us finish eating fell on deaf ears. This person was indeed a tough lady, who was unbending in her desire to get us out of there.

I should mention that this group of people and their Newfs had travelled various distances to be there for this event. Some lived a couple of miles away, but others had driven up to two hours to be there. What were we to do? Ingrid and I just happened to live closest to the park, so we volunteered to have everyone over to our house to continue our celebration. I cannot imagine what our neighbours across the creek were thinking when we showed up at home followed by a convoy of vehicles loaded with approximately ten to fifteen people and eight to ten Newfs. Needless to say, our deck and backyard were in chaos for the afternoon, but everyone had a great time. It is strange, but I don't remember our neighbours ever mentioning that to us.

Rim on a visit with nina and marc

newf baseball lineup

A very wet picnic, but look at those smiles!

These guys didn't even notice the downpour

Fran with molly's mom, Goldie (Rainbows End)

Here is Lars-a happy man-and a contented newf

Keith—a man with everything under control
(until a cat strolls by)

Tina with Caera, Misha and our four-treats
in the fields

nina with molly's dad, marcarpents maneen

marij geocaching with naja

molly and father, maneen, at Canadian Specialty

keith with molly's sister, Georgy, and mom, Goldie—
a nova Scotia holiday

Newfs As Protectors

Regardless of their gentleness, friendliness and overall "teddy bear" qualities, these dogs can have their moments that restore an owner's confidence that his Newf will go the distance in protecting him when necessary. Molly is one of the gentlest dogs we have ever met. She goes out of her way to lick any dog or person who ventures within range. She will willingly roll over onto her back to expose herself for belly rubs to anyone willing to accommodate her. So it was a surprise indeed when one day she showed another side of her personality.

It was a summer day, late in the afternoon, when I was busy in the backyard of our home. The four dogs were lying around in the shade of the trees, either watching what I was doing or snoring so loudly it was as if they were trying to drown out the noise of the birds in the trees or the bullfrogs croaking in the creek. I was not able to see the driveway at the front of the house, so when I heard one of the Newfs barking up on the front deck, I went to see what was happening. I found Molly standing there, barking and looking up the driveway to the road. Parked at the end of our driveway was a small dilapidated car, and I could make out four men, two in the front, two in the back. They were parked on our road but across the opening of the driveway.

We live in a very small, very rural community, and traffic on our small road is limited to the few residents and their visitors, and because we live quite far from our nearest neighbour, a car stopped at our house is very rare. Molly's barking was a normal bark, ostensibly to let me know that someone was coming to visit. I stood beside her and put my hand on her back to let her know that everything was okay, and she stopped barking. We both stood there watching the car, waiting for someone to get out. As the minutes passed and nothing happened, I started to wonder what was going on and began feeling a little apprehensive. It was almost five minutes before one of the back doors opened and a large, ominous looking person got out. He started walking slowly up the driveway to the gated deck where Molly and I were standing. He had his head down and looked quite strange. I called to him, asking what he wanted, but he ignored me and just kept approaching, still with his head down. At this point I started to feel quite nervous about this. Immediately Molly changed from our teddy bear Newf to a very ferocious sounding monster Newf. The barking was no longer an advisement that someone was here but a very loud, violent warning for this person to leave. This time I did not stop her from barking. As he approached closer, I asked again what he wanted. Again, he did not answer; nor did he raise his head. He simply dropped our new telephone directory on the driveway, turned and went back to the car. These four delivery men continued down the street delivering the rest of their telephone directories.

This was an innocent incident that occurs thousands of times in communities everywhere. But this guy was not acting normally. He was giving off strange, scary signals, and as soon as I started feeling nervous, Molly picked it up right away and made her transformation from licky, cuddly Newfie to ferocious protector of her "pack." I do not know what would have happened if

125

there had been no gate between us, but Newfs are known to use their size and strength to protect rather than physically attacking someone. We unquestionably feel safe in our home with these four patrolling the premises.

naming Conventions

naming dogs is often a topic of conversation among dog owners. Some choose common dogs names like Rex and Rover. Others use their imagination to come up with unique, sometimes unusual names. In the past we fell into the former category, but during the past few years, we have migrated to using more creative names.

Murphy was our first Newf, and when he came to us at eight weeks of age we thought long and hard about an appropriate name for this "giant to be." Ingrid's favourite actor is James Garner and her favourite actress is Sally Field. In which movie did they star together? *Murphy's Romance.*

We rescued Bailey, our second Newf, from an animal shelter. His name at the time was Billy. Even though most often I am known as Bill, I have certain family members, sister Margaret for example, who have always called me Billy (much to my chagrin). One Billy in the house is enough, so to prevent any confusion as to who is being sent outside to pee in the middle of the night, we renamed him Bailey. He was four years old at the time, and Bailey sounds a lot like Billy so was less confusing for him.

Our third Newf was Enchantee. She came to us at four years old. She was named by the breeder, and I can only guess that she was named for her enchanting personality.

Next came Molly. Her full registered name is Molly of the Blue. We chose this name for two reasons. Molly was also the name of one of Nina Cote's older Newfs who was a lovable old girl of thirteen years. So Molly was named after her. The rest of her name, "of the Blue," was chosen to reflect the fact that she is a Newf and loves water.

Seven came to live with us from the breeder when she was five years old. She was named Seven of Nine because she was the seventh girl in a litter of nine pups. He denies it, but I still think Nina's hubby, Marc, had in mind the Star Trek character Seven of Nine.

Rimshot is the son of a very impressive male in Marcarpents Kennels of years ago. He was imported from Norway, and his name was Drummer. *Rimshot* is a drumming term that refers to striking the edge of the drum with the drumstick. Something like saying he is like his dad—a chip off the old block.

Annie (full name L'il Orphan Annie) was so named because when she and her littermates were three weeks old, they lost their mom to an unfortunate accident. Because of that they had to be put on solid food earlier than normal and enjoyed some human "mothering."

The Wonders of Dog Therapy

Years ago, when we had Murphy and Bailey, I was making semi-annual trips to New Brunswick to visit my mom, who was in a long-term care facility. On a lot of these trips I would take Bailey along with me, because Mom always loved these big dogs, so a visit from both her son and Bailey was indeed a high point. Bailey would accompany me to her room, and we would all spend great afternoons together. During one of these visits, the attendants brought in a lady in a wheelchair to see the "big dog." This lady was in her nineties and had been at the facility for a couple of months but had yet to communicate to anyone. She was angry that she had to be there so refused to talk to anyone and kept to herself. The staff wheeled her into Mom's room and sat her on the chesterfield. Bailey, who had been lying on the other side of the room next to Mom, immediately got up and went to see this lady. He laid his huge head on her lap and waited for a scratch. The lady started petting his head and smiled. Within minutes she was talking to us all, telling us about dogs she had known in her life. The staff was shocked, and we were introduced to dog therapy.

This was our first experience with dog therapy, even though it was not intended. Now, years later, we had four Newfs, I was retired, and thoughts of dog therapy came back. We decided to attempt to have Molly and Rimshot officially certified in this field. We chose an organization by the name of TPOC (Therapeutic Paws of Canada) to perform the necessary testing. The day came, and we all gathered in a gymnasium at a local church for the event. Along with Molly and Rimshot there were six other dogs also trying for this distinction. Dogs and handlers were lined up along one wall of the gym, and one by one a dog and handler were called to the centre for a specific test. They then would return to their spot along the wall to await the next one. Molly, of course, would greet and lick every dog as she or he returned to the wall, as if to say, "You did great" or "I did great, eh?"

There are twelve tests to determine if the dog is calm and friendly enough to fit in a hospital or nursing home environment and to make sure it would get along with other dogs (no problem for Molly). Rimshot and Molly both passed, and they started on their new careers as therapy dogs.

Rimshot just before his retirement from therapy

For the past three years we have been working with children with reading problems and with Alzheimer's patients and other seniors. The reading program is in conjunction with the local chapter of the Literacy Council, and Rimshot is the founding dog in the "Read to Rimshot" program. In this program children with reading problems are brought into a room with the dog, and they sit on a pillow on the floor with the dog and read to him. Studies in the United States and Canada have shown that the fact that the dog is non-judgmental encourages the child to read. These studies also show that a stressed child shows a marked decrease in blood pressure simply from touching the dog while reading. We have had several parents come to us after the sessions and tell us that they have never seen their child read so well. Sessions are held weekly at the Literacy Council building during after-school hours.

Our work with Alzheimer's patients and other seniors has been equally rewarding. For the past two years we have been visiting a local long-term care facility by the name of Glen Stor Dun Lodge. Here we have met many enthusiastic residents and staff who have grown to know our dogs and eagerly anticipate their weekly visits. Both Molly and Rimshot seem to fit right into this environment. They both become noticeably excited as soon as they realize where they are going and eagerly pull us through the door into the facility. They have forged strong bonds with many of the residents, who look forward to the "dog visits." We have had several instances where caregivers have been rather surprised at the reactions of some. Residents who seldom communicate suddenly become quite talkative when the dogs are around. One lady with advanced Alzheimer's spends most her day either in her room or in a sitting area with other residents, with minimum amount of communication. However, when we bring one of the dogs to her floor, she becomes very active, lots of smiling, and follows us everywhere we go, from room to room. When we leave the floor, we must have one of the staff with us so she doesn't follow us onto the elevator.

Tyler is also starting to join us on our dog therapy excursions. He will tour the facility with me, meeting residents and staff, and will explain all about the Newfoundland dog to those who are interested. This has shown him another side of the dogs. He now sees how they sense the "need" in some people and thus how they are able to benefit others.

molly bringing smiles to those around her

Rimshot is now eleven years old and is starting to feel his age, so we have had to cut back on his therapy work. He now is better suited to the reading program, because he does not have to do any walking but rather sits with the kids while they read. This is fine with him, and the children, most of whom have been reading to him for two or more years, love it when Rimshot shows up. They particularly like it when he falls asleep during the reading and snores. He snores quite loudly, and the first time that happened we had people coming in from adjoining classrooms to see what the noise was. Ever since then, some of the kids reading to him try to get him to fall asleep, just to hear him snore. This is fine with us because we are always looking for ways to encourage reading, so it all works out.

Molly has picked up the slack with the Alzheimer's work, and Annie is in the process of being trained, as there is a lot more work to be done. Until recently, Seven had not been involved with therapy work because she has a strong aversion to elevators and tight closed-in spaces. However we have just started working at a new facility that has one level and wide, spacious hallways. Seven is now in training and enjoying the work. In fact, I was quite surprised when I took her in to this facility for her second visit. She fit into the routine as if she had been doing it for years. She seemed to know exactly what she had to do. When I go into a room with Molly or Rim, we enter the room together, and the dog waits until I indicate that he or she is to greet the resident. The dog will then approach. Seven, however, confidently marches through that door into the room or meeting area and immediately makes her way to the resident, stops in front of him and either lays her head in his lap or looks up into his eyes as if saying, "Well, here I am; feel free to scratch these ears and shower me with attention." During this second visit, she quickly became the favourite of everyone with whom she came in contact. She is going to be a very good ambassador of the breed in this therapy work.

The dogs still amaze us in many ways. At home or at play they most often are goofy and playful, but at therapy they take on a much more serious attitude, as if they really do understand what is expected of them.

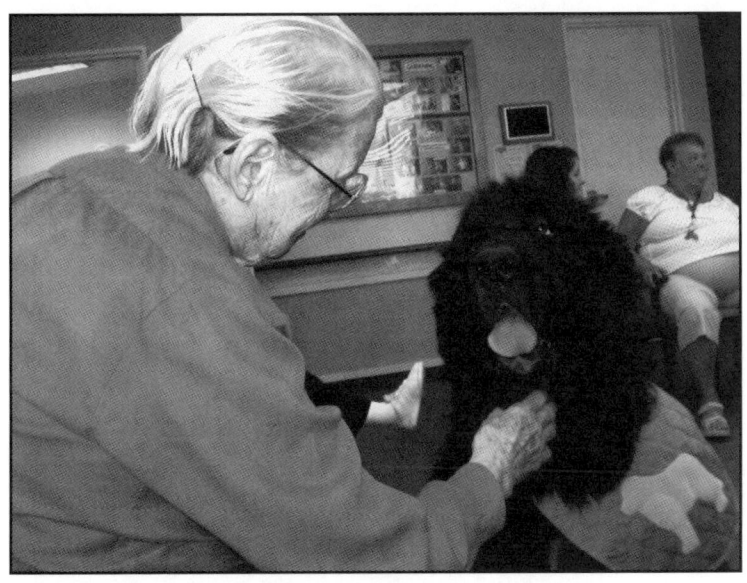

molly loving the attention

annie's first time

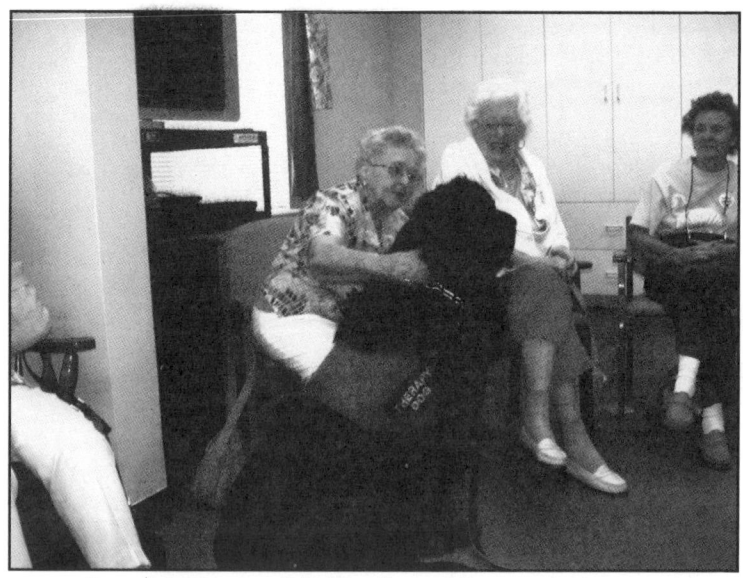

molly doing her "thing," making people happy

Rim catching a nap during the reading with Samantha

With therapy dogs it is most important to maintain a high degree of socialization. Therefore, as often as possible, we take one or two dogs with us when we go somewhere. One of the best environments for a dog to be socialized is at a crowded mall. The size and colour of the Newfoundland usually makes a big hit with adults and children alike. This results in closed-in, noisy situations, which are most beneficial for a therapy dog. During one such visit to an indoor mall, I had Molly with me, and we were standing in line at a Tim Horton's for coffee. As usual, most everyone in the line was talking about and asking questions about this large beast. One gentleman showed a keen interest in this therapy work we were doing and introduced himself as a managing editor of the city newspaper. He took my name and told me that he would like to do a human interest story about these Newfs and the work that they do.

Last week we were contacted by a reporter from the paper, who conducted a forty-minute interview by telephone and then asked to meet me with the two certified Newfs at the mall for a photo shoot. The next afternoon I entered the mall with Molly and Rimshot and discovered that because of spring break, the mall was unusually packed with people. Having these two huge dogs therefore resulted in large crowds of adults, school-aged kids and toddlers gathering around. Walking from one place to another was extremely difficult. However, this was the ideal situation for the dogs and is exactly the reason we bring them to these places.

At one point I was standing, both dogs were lying on the floor, and we were surrounded by twenty to thirty of the curious. Tiny children were sitting on the floor, dwarfed by the huge dogs, and everyone with smiles on their faces. Through the crowd I noticed a fellow with a camera bending and twisting in all types of contorted positions, taking picture after picture, also with a smile on his face. This was the photographer, who obviously had no problem in locating me in the mall. The session lasted for about forty-five minutes, many photos were taken, and the children spent much of the time with wide smiles on their faces. The article appeared the next day in the paper, and we had made page two. The next weekend at our regularly scheduled visit to the retirement home, almost everyone we met had seen the article, and Molly was received as a star.

Bonnie with Samantha reading to Rimshot

Corey reading to an interested Rimshot

EPILOGUE

It must be apparent from reading this book that it is a challenge to own four Newfoundland dogs. Their lifespan is not as long as that of the smaller breeds, so the sorrow of losing one seems to come quickly, and then there are the slime and shedding factors, which can be daunting. Why do we endure all this to have these dogs? The reason is simply because they give so much while they are with us. Complete devotion and loyalty to their owners are amazing qualities for any dog or other animal. These characteristics just happen to be inherent in the Newfoundland. Although gentleness, caring and sensitivity to seniors and small children is a quality present in some other breeds, we have found that they are common in Newfoundlands. There has never been a moment when we have regretted our decision to involve them in our life and spend our time among the giants.